MACHINES RULE!

ON THE SEA

Steve Parker

W

FRANKLIN WATTS

LONDON • SYDNEY

This edition 2012

First published in 2008
by Franklin Watts

Copyright © Franklin Watts 2008

Franklin Watts
338 Euston Road
London NW1 3BH

Franklin Watts Australia
Level 17/207 Kent Street
Sydney, NSW 2000

A CIP catalogue record for this book
is available from the British Library.

Dewey number: 623.8

ISBN 978 1 4451 0931 2

Printed in China

Franklin Watts is a division of
Hachette Children's Books,
an Hachette Livre UK company.

Editor: Jeremy Smith
Editor-in-chief: John C. Miles
Design: Billin Design Solutions
Art director: Jonathan Hair

Picture credits: Aston Martin: 6, 10,
11r, 11br. Bugatti: OFC, 4-5, 8-9.
Corbis/Bruce Benedict/Transtock:
11b. Ducatti: 19c & b. istockphoto:
OFC bl & br, 7t, 7c, 7b, 12 all, 13t,
13b, 22 all, 23t, 23b, 24 all, 25c.
www.JayOhrberg.com: 13c.
Shutterstock: 11t, 14b, 14t, 15c,
15b, 16, 17 all, 19t, 20-21 all, 23tr,
25 all, 26-27 all, 28-29 all.

Franklin Watts is a division of
Hachette Children's Books, an
Hachette UK company.

www.hachette.co.uk

CONTENTS

On the sea

From a tiny rowing boat to a giant supertanker, the water is a great place to be. People enjoy their canoes, sailing dinghies, speedboats, yachts, luxury motor cruisers and other leisure craft. The sea is also home to large vessels that carry goods across vast distances, and military boats that protect countries from attack.

Fun on the water

Jetskis and powerboats are great fun at sea. In the right hands, they can zoom across the water, and perform amazing stunts.

Passenger ships

Many people go on holiday by boat. Vessels including hovercraft and **hydrofoils** skim across the water at high speeds, while cruise liners take you to your destination in style.

Giant ships

Huge container ships and **supertankers** carry loads for thousands of kilometres across the water. Countries protect their shores using giant military ships that bristle with weapons.

Private luxury

Some rich people like to travel across the water in luxury. Private yachts and motorcraft costing millions of pounds show real style at sea.

Offshore powerboat

It's rough, tough, fast, furious – and very wet! Huge waves batter the boat, wind and spray sting your face, and opponents try to speed past. P1 powerboating is like Formula 1 car racing, as the best challenge the rest.

Powerboats speed through choppy water at great speed. The boat's **hull** has to be strong enough to stand up to powerful waves.

strong hull

Stats and Facts

P1 Evolution class powerboat racer

Makers: Various

Length: 11-13.1 metres

Width: 2.5-3.5 metres

Height: 2-3 metres

Weight: 4.2 tonnes

Crew: Up to 3

Engines: Up to 13 litres diesel, 11 litres petrol

Top speed: 160 km/h

magnetic compass

dials and displays

steering wheel

Two huge **marine** diesel engines sit in the rear of the hull.

outboard motor provides power

The jetski or PWC, personal watercraft, is a combination of a motorbike and fast boat for racing across the sea. You can do stunts like loops, surf the waves, tow a water-skier, chase sharks, or just have great fun!

The jetski has handlebars for steering, like a motorbike. Acceleration in a jetski is provided by a hand-powered throttle located on the right-side grip. By twisting the throttle, the driver can increase power to the motor.

THAT'S INCREDIBLE

Jetski freestylers ride backwards, somersault in mid air, and even go underwater and then shoot up high into the air like a leaping dolphin.

Stats and Facts

Freestyle jetskiers invent their own stunts!

Kawasaki STX-15F

Maker: Kawasaki

Length: 3.1 metres

Width: 1.2 metres

Height: 1.05 metres

Dry weight: 330 kg

Crew: Rider, 2 passengers

Engines: 1.5 litre 4-cylinder petrol

Top speed: 105-plus km/h

Jetski competitions are held all around the world. Riders earn points by twisting and turning around buoys and performing stunts.

Supercarrier

The supercarrier is a floating city built for war. Apart from providing a base for jet fighters and helicopters, it is also armed with its own missiles, guns, torpedoes and other weapons. And it bristles with radio aerials and radar to detect the enemy.

Supersized aircraft carriers are among the world's biggest ships. The deck is wide and flat, and the **bridge** (control room) tower is on one side, so planes can take off and land.

With an ear-splitting roar, the plane takes off from the **deck** into the air.

Stats and Facts

THAT'S INCREDIBLE

You could fit four football pitches onto the deck of a supercarrier – but you'd lose a lot of footballs overboard!

Patrol aircraft on board the supercarrier.

Nimitz Class Supercarrier

Nation: USA

Length: 333 metres

Width: 76 metres

Weight: 91,000 tonnes

Crew: 3,200 carrier, 2,500 aircraft

Aircraft: 90

Engines: 2 A4W nuclear reactors, 4 steam turbines

Top speed: 56-plus km/h

Radar screens show the position of ships and aircraft in the area.

13

Nuclear attack sub

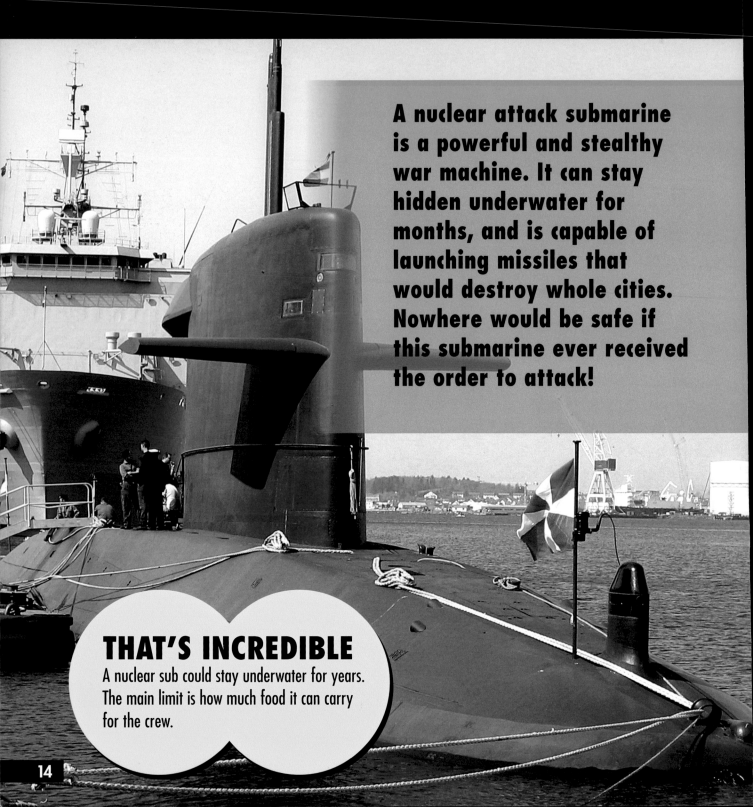

A nuclear attack submarine is a powerful and stealthy war machine. It can stay hidden underwater for months, and is capable of launching missiles that would destroy whole cities. Nowhere would be safe if this submarine ever received the order to attack!

THAT'S INCREDIBLE

A nuclear sub could stay underwater for years. The main limit is how much food it can carry for the crew.

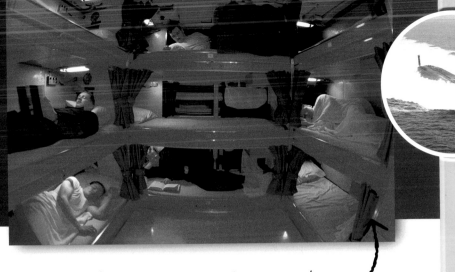

Space on board is cramped, so you have to get on with other crew members!

Seawolf Class SSN21

Maker: USA

Length: 108 metres

Width: 12.2 metres

Weight: 9,140 tonnes

Crew: 116

Engine: GE PWR S6W nuclear reactor

Top speed: 65 km/h underwater

Dive depth: 610 metres

The commander and crew watch the **sonar** screen and other displays to check their position in the vast, dark ocean.

A tall telescope called a **periscope** sticks above the surface to let the crew see above the water.

15

Supertanker

The biggest ships in the world are huge oil tankers. They carry crude oil (petroleum) from remote oilfields to busy ports and cities. The oil is turned into hundreds of products we use every day, from petrol to plastics to paints.

The bridge and control equipment, and the rooms where the crew relax, eat and sleep, are all near the rear of the supertanker. They are above the main deck, allowing room for giant oil tanks below.

If a tanker is damaged, thick black crude petroleum leaks out as an oil **slick**. This causes terrible damage to sea and shore life.

Knock Nevis (formerly known as *Seawise Giant, Jahre Viking*)

Maker: Sumitomo, Japan

Length: 458 metres

Width: 69 metres

Draft: 25 metres

Weight: 564,000 tonnes

Crew: 40

Engines: 1 steam turbine producing 50,000 HP

Top speed: 24 km/h

THAT'S INCREDIBLE

In 1975, the biggest ever supertanker, the *Seawise Giant,* was built. In 1999, it was relaunched as the *Jahre Viking,* and in 2004, it was refitted again and became the *Knock Nevis.*

Container ships carry goods in piles of steel container boxes.

Hovercraft

Hovercraft float like a boat when still. When the large propellers in the hull called lifting fans start up, however, the craft rises up on an air cushion. It is then powered along the water by propellers at the back.

back propellers

air cushion

hull

Smaller hovercraft work as **ferries** across rivers and between islands, taking people and goods quickly across the water.

Large hovercraft are used to carry hundreds of cars across the water.

Stats and Facts

Solent Express

Maker: Hoverwork/ Hovertravel

Length: 29 metres

Width: 14 metres

Weight: 70 tonnes

Passengers: 130

Engines: Diesel

Top speed: 90-plus km/h

Navies use giant hovercraft as landing craft. These vehicles are at home on land and sea, and can bring troops and tanks onto the beach.

THAT'S INCREDIBLE

The biggest passenger hovercraft, the SRN4 Mk3, is more than 50 metres long, weighs over 300 tonnes, and can carry over 400 passengers - and 60 cars!

rudder

A hovercraft is steered using a flat blade called the rudder.

Hydros and cats

A hydrofoil is a ship on stilts. It has struts that hold it up on underwater wings called foils, so it can go faster. Catamarans are multi-hulls, with two main parts in the water instead of the usual one.

As the hydrofoil gains speed, its **foils** make a lifting force, like aircraft wings. This pushes the main hull above the water. The foils tilt to adjust the lift force.

foils

FAIRLIGHT

Passengers relax as the hydrofoil skims through the waves. →

Stats and Facts

PS-30 Jetfoil

Maker: Shanghai Simno Marine, China

Length: 27.8 metres

Width: 8.6 metres

Draught: 4.5 metres, strut down

Weight: 303 tonnes

Passengers: 260

Engines: 2 Rolls Royce Allison 501-KF gas turbines

Top speed: 80-plus km/h

The fastest hydrofoil can travel at over 90 km/h.

THAT'S INCREDIBLE

Team Philips, the world's biggest catamaran yacht, cost $4 million when it was launched in 2000. A few months later it broke up and sank in a storm.

Huge catamarans carry hundreds of people on fast ferry rides. They tilt less from side to side than single-hulled boats (monohulls).

Cruiseliner

This giant hotel has cafes, restaurants, bars, cinemas, gyms, swimming pools, games rooms – and it floats! The luxury cruise liner is the finest way to travel and visit exotic countries around the world.

Take a dip in the floodlit pool as the fountains spray and the stars twinkle overhead.

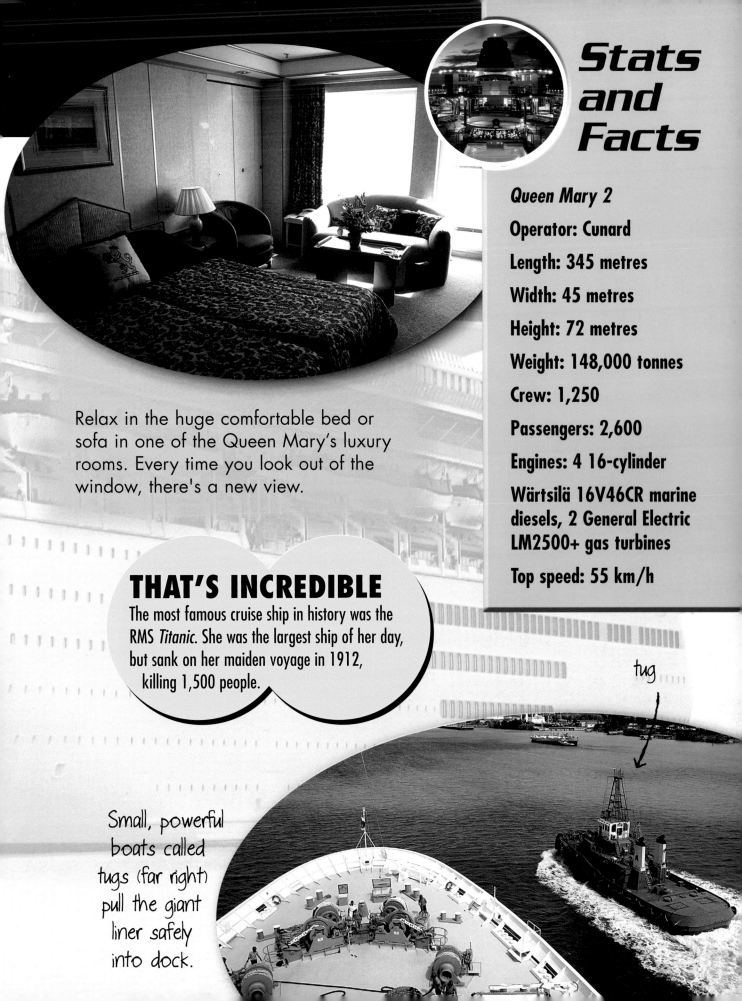

Stats and Facts

Queen Mary 2

Operator: Cunard

Length: 345 metres

Width: 45 metres

Height: 72 metres

Weight: 148,000 tonnes

Crew: 1,250

Passengers: 2,600

Engines: 4 16-cylinder

Wärtsilä 16V46CR marine diesels, 2 General Electric LM2500+ gas turbines

Top speed: 55 km/h

Relax in the huge comfortable bed or sofa in one of the Queen Mary's luxury rooms. Every time you look out of the window, there's a new view.

THAT'S INCREDIBLE

The most famous cruise ship in history was the RMS *Titanic*. She was the largest ship of her day, but sank on her maiden voyage in 1912, killing 1,500 people.

tug

Small, powerful boats called tugs (far right) pull the giant liner safely into dock.

Luxury motorcraft

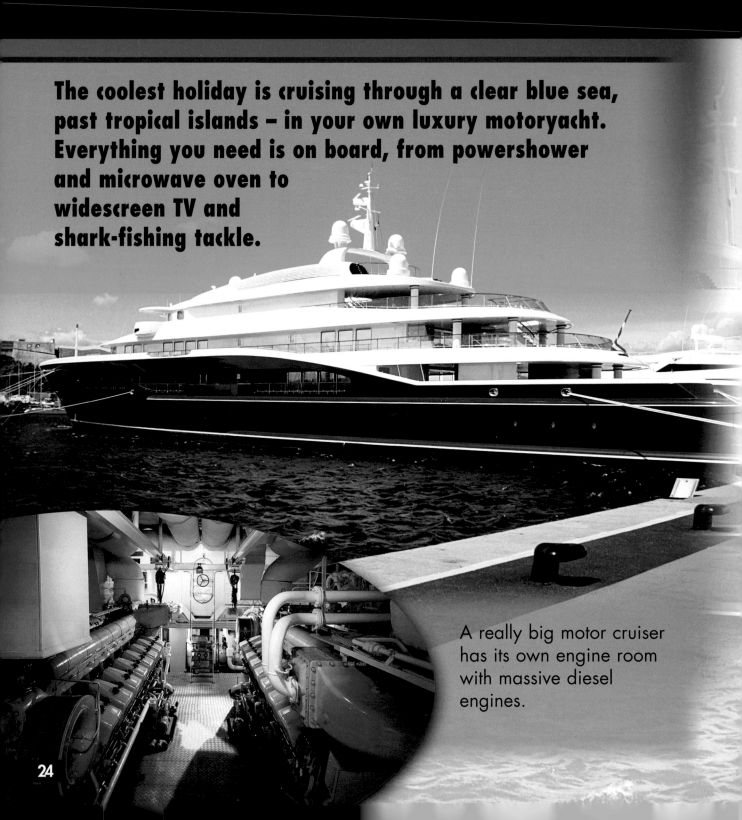

The coolest holiday is cruising through a clear blue sea, past tropical islands – in your own luxury motoryacht. Everything you need is on board, from powershower and microwave oven to widescreen TV and shark-fishing tackle.

A really big motor cruiser has its own engine room with massive diesel engines.

Stats and Facts

THAT'S INCREDIBLE

To hire a private yacht usually costs at least £1,000 per hour. That's cheaper than buying one at around £5 million!

Pearl 50

Maker: Pearl Motor Yachts

Length: 15 metres

Width: 4.4 metres

Draft: 1.4 metres

Sleeps: Up to 6

Engines: 2 Volvo D9

500HP diesels

Top speed: 55 km/h

Equipment: Electric sunroof, barbecue, electric patio door, dishwasher as standard

Big motorcruisers carry 20 or more guests.

The main lounge has every comfort, especially for rainy, windy days when it is too cold to sunbathe on deck.

The streamlined hull is made of fibreglass.

Ocean-racing yacht

If you want a month of incredibly hard work, rough conditions, seasickness, few comforts and no luxury – how about an ocean yacht race? The crew fight winds, waves and currents to stay on course, all day and night.

THAT'S INCREDIBLE

The Volvo Round the World Yacht Race covers a total of more than 55,000 kilometres.

At the start line, yachts crowd together to try and 'steal the wind' from each other. Their balloon-like **spinnaker** sails fill, and soon they will spread out across the vast, lonely ocean.

Stats and Facts

As the yacht's sails fill with wind, it tilts over. The crew leans to the other side to keep it going straight.

Ericsson 70 Class Round-the-World Yacht 2006

Maker: Various

Length: 21.5 metres

Width: 5.7 metres

Height: Mast top 31.5 metres above water

Weight: 14 tonnes

Main sail area: 172 square metres

Spinnaker area: 500 square metres

Top speed: 55-plus km/h

dials showing wind and water speed

steering wheel operates rudder

boom

rigging

The crew climb, clamber and scramble among the **masts** and **booms**, and pull on the **rigging** (ropes) to adjust the sails.

Glossary

Boom

On a yacht or sailing ship one of the horizontal poles that holds out the sails.

Bridge

The main control room of a ship or boat, where the captain and crew steer the vessel and watch for problems.

Compass

On a ship or boat, an instrument used for finding directions. The needle always points to the magnetic North.

Container ship

A large ship that carries big metal boxes with doors, called containers, which can be lifted by cranes and loaded onto trucks or railway wagons.

Deck

A fairly wide, flat part of a ship, where people can move about. Some big ships have more than 10 decks.

Dock

A place where ships park.

Ferry

A ship or boat carrying people, cars and other loads on regular trips between two or three places.

Fibreglass

A very light, strong material made of strands of glass-like fibre material within a plastic-type resin.

Foils

On a hydrofoil, the narrow strips on struts that slice through the water, making a lifting force to raise the vessel above the surface.

Hull

The main body of a ship or boat, with smooth streamlined sides that taper to a narrow point at the front.

Hydrofoil

A boat that rises above the surface on strip-like foils mounted on struts or legs.

Marine

To do with the sea, such as marine diesel engines, which are specially designed to power ships and boats.

Mast

On a ship or boat, a tall pole that holds up radio aerials and other items, and the sails on a sailing ship or yacht.

Outboard

Outside of the main hull, such as an outboard motor.

Periscope

A bent telescope that can look around corners or see above an object.

Propeller

Angled blades that spin around, like a windmill, to push along a water vessel or

aircraft. In a boat they are also called screws.

Rigging

The ropes, cords and other lines that hold sails up and out, or let them be lowered and folded or furled.

Radar

A device that locates objects using sound.

Rudder

A vertical blade at the stern of a vessel that can be turned horizontally to change the vessel's direction when in motion.

Slick

When fluid such as engine oil, crude oil (petroleum) or a chemical leaks out of a vessel and causes damage.

Sonar

Sending out sound waves to bounce off objects, then detecting the returning echoes to find the direction, distance and size of the object. Sonar stands for Sound Navigation And Ranging.

Spinnaker

The large-balloon sail used by some kinds of yachts.

Tug

A small, very powerful boat that pulls or pushes much bigger boats into and out of harbours and other tight places.

Find out more

http://library.thinkquest.org/04oct/00450/ridingwaves.htm
Water transport with ships, boats and sails, and links to many other pages about different kinds of vessels.

http://www.arthropolis.com/links/boatship.htm
Lots of stories and interesting facts about ships and boats

http://www.powerboatp1.com/
Home website of the World P1 Powerboat Racing Championships.

http://www.explainthatstuff.com/hovercraft.html
All about hovercraft and hydrofoils, including how they work, their history and uses.

http://www.speedrecordclub.com/outwater.php
List of the fastest people ever over water.

Further reading

Ships (Amazing Machines) by Chris Oxlade, Franklin Watts 2006

Ships (War Machines) by Simon Adams, Franklin Watts 2008

Speedboats (Now That's Fast!) by Kate Riggs, Franklin Watts 2011

Note to parents and teachers:

Every effort has been made by the Publishers to ensure that the websites in this book are suitable for children, that they are of the highest educational value, and that they contain no inappropriate or offensive material. However, because of the nature of the Internet, it is impossible to guarantee that the contents of these sites will not be altered. We strongly advise that Internet access is supervised by a responsible adult.

Index